My Science Library

Studying Our Earth, Inside and Out

Kimberly M. Hutmacher

Science Content Editor:
Shirley Duke

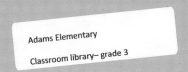

Rourke
Educational Media

rourkeeducationalmedia.com

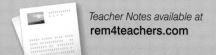

Teacher Notes available at
rem4teachers.com

Science Content Editor: Shirley Duke holds a bachelor's degree in biology and a master's degree in education from Austin College in Sherman, Texas. She taught science in Texas at all levels for twenty-five years before starting to write for children. Her science books include *You Can't Wear These Genes, Infections, Infestations, and Diseases, Enterprise STEM, Forces and Motion at Work, Environmental Disasters,* and *Gases*. She continues writing science books and also works as a science content editor.

www.rourkeeducationalmedia.com

Photo credits: Cover © Andrea Danti, alin b., Christopher Ewing; Pages 2/3 © Matt Antonino; Pages 4/5 © zzoplanet, pio3; Pages 6/7 © TranceDrumer; Pages 8/9 © Mopic, Matt Antonino, Andrea Danti; Pages 10/11 © Qfl247, beboy; Pages 12/13 © Ocean and Design, Christian Lopetz, Ikluft; Pages 14/15 © Anthro, Christopher Eng-Wong Photography; Pages 16/17 © Miao Liao; Pages 18/19 © Santi Rodriguez; Pages 20/21 © IKO, Heide Hellebrand

Editor: Kelli Hicks

My Science Library series produced by Blue Door Publishing, Florida for Rourke Educational Media.

Library of Congress PCN Data

Hutmacher, Kimberly M.
 Studying Our Earth, Inside and Out / Kimberly M. Hutmacher.
    p. cm. -- (My Science Library)
 ISBN 978-1-61810-091-7 (Hard cover) (alk. paper)
 ISBN 978-1-61810-224-9 (Soft cover)
 Library of Congress Control Number: 2011943577

Rourke Educational Media
Printed in the United States of America,
North Mankato, Minnesota

Rourke
Educational Media

rourkeeducationalmedia.com

customerservice@rourkeeducationalmedia.com
PO Box 643328 Vero Beach, Florida 32964

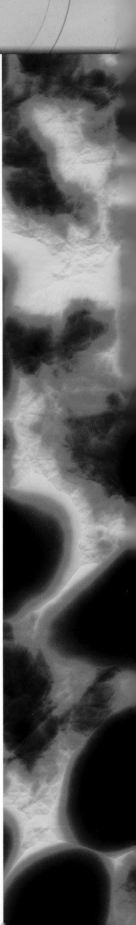

Table of Contents

Our Amazing Earth

We live on amazing planet Earth, and one of the things that makes Earth so amazing is us! Earth is the only planet known to support human life. Let's take a closer look at Earth, both inside and out.

More Amazing Facts:

Earth is the fifth largest planet and is home to over 8 million species.

Sun

Earth

Earth is nicknamed the Blue Planet because 70 percent of it is covered in water.

Peeling Back Earth's Layers

Earth has a **crust**, **mantle**, and **core**. How do we know this? Our information comes from **geologists**, scientists who study Earth.

Earth's outer layer is called the crust. This is the rocky layer of Earth which is covered by the dirt and grass in our backyards. Mountains and land under the oceans are part of the Earth's crust.

Schilthorn Mountain in Switzerland is part of the crust that has been pushed upward by crustal plate movement.

Below Earth's crust is a thick layer of hot, semi-solid rock called the upper and lower mantle. Beneath the mantle is Earth's core. The outer core is made up mostly of heated liquid iron while the inner core is mainly solid iron.

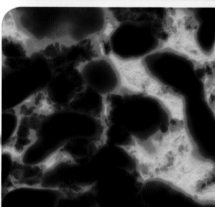

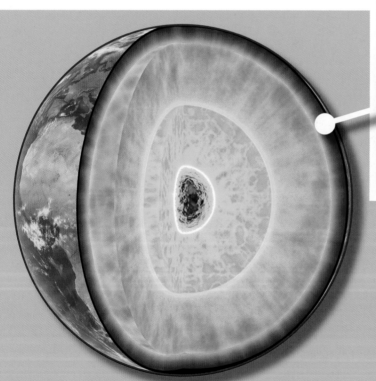

Heat from the core melts the rocks, forming the mantle.

The hot, slowly moving rock inside the mantle carries heat upward inside the Earth as it rises. It meets the crust, causing earthquakes in the stiffer crust.

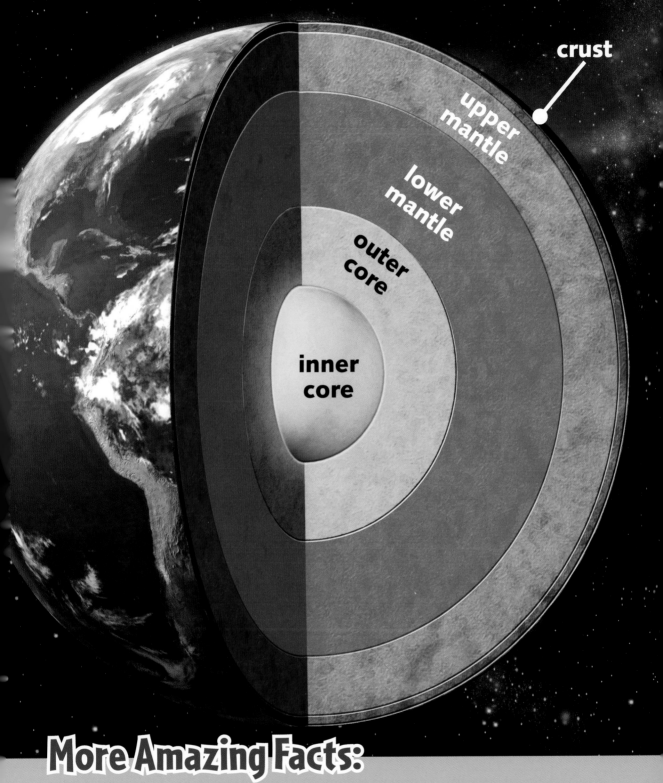

crust

upper mantle

lower mantle

outer core

inner core

More Amazing Facts:

The thickness of the Earth's crust varies. Under the oceans, the crust averages about 4 miles (6.4 km) thick. Continental crust is thicker. It averages about 19 miles (30 km) thick and can be as thick as 37 miles (60 km) in mountain ranges. The mantle is about 1,800 miles (2,900 km) thick.

Scientists study Earth to gather information for different reasons. Geologists study Earth's crust to get an accurate picture of its history and the forces that shaped it. Seismologists study information gathered about Earth's structure in order to locate earthquakes and faults.

Information gathered by geologists is used in construction, environmental planning, and locating natural resources like coal, petroleum, and natural gas.

Volcanologists study active volcanoes and collect samples of gases trapped beneath Earth's hardened **lava**. They use information gathered from these samples to help predict future volcanic activity.

As well as collecting gas samples, volcanologists collect samples of ash, rock, and lava.

Magma from the mantle is forced up a chimney-shaped vent by pressure and gases in the molten rock miles below the Earth. It bursts out of the crater and flows down the cone of the volcano.

A Giant Jigsaw Puzzle

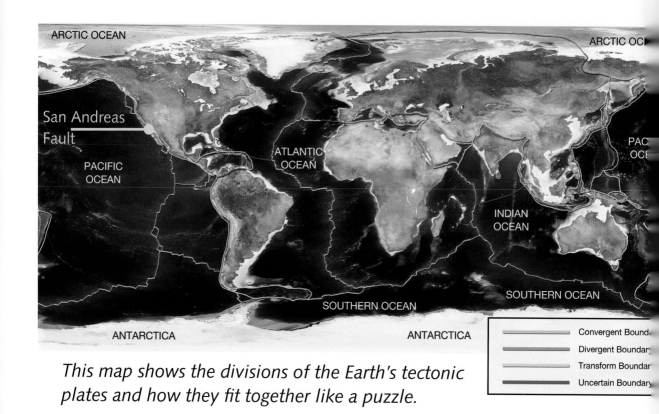

This map shows the divisions of the Earth's tectonic plates and how they fit together like a puzzle.

Earth's crust is broken up into many pieces called **plates**. The plates fit together like a giant jigsaw puzzle!

Fault lines mark a boundary between two tectonic plates. The most famous fault in the United States, the San Andreas fault, is located where two tectonic plates meet, the North American and Pacific.

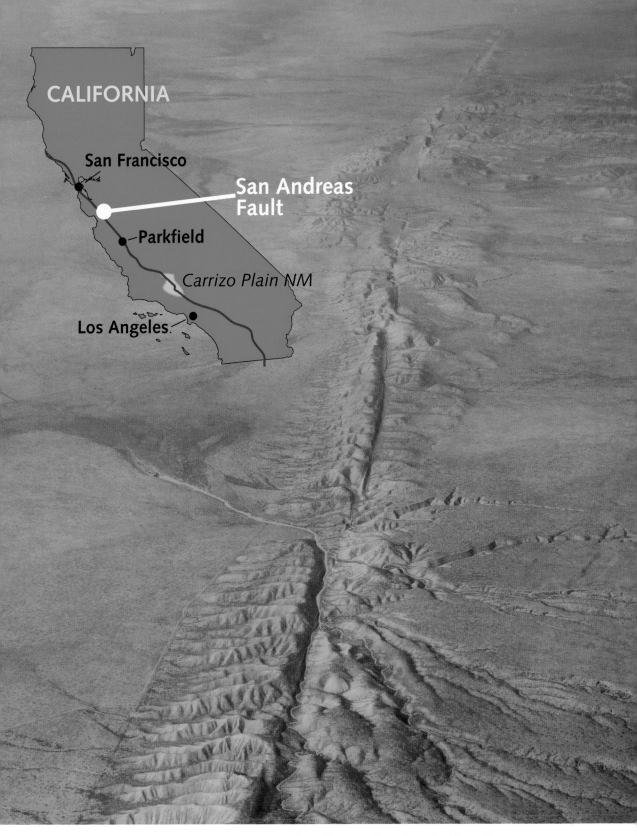

The San Andreas fault is an example of a strike-slip fault. The two plate boundaries are sliding past the other and get hung up. When they release, the sudden motion causes an earthquake.

Sculpting Earth

Earth's land and waterways are always changing. Earth's plates crash and slide, forcing one under the other in slow motion. Over time, the folded crust pushes up, forming a mountain range.

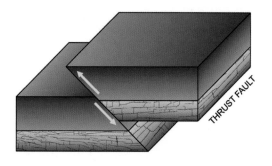

THRUST FAULT

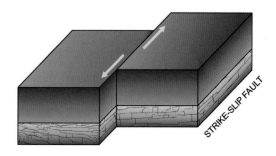

STRIKE-SLIP FAULT

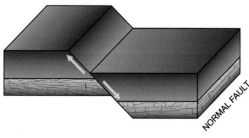

NORMAL FAULT

Fault lines mark a boundary between two tectonic plates. Shifting fault lines and plates have created and continue to shape Earth's landforms.

This is one of over 100,000 glaciers located in Alaska. It may sound like a large amount, but glaciers only cover about five percent of the state.

Moving water changes Earth's shape. Layers of snow build at the tops of mountains to form giant sheets of ice called **glaciers**. As glaciers slide down, over millions of years, they scrape away rock, sculpting deep valleys.

Muddy water carrying sand, soil, and gravel chisels away at solid rock, slicing and shaping deep **canyons**.

A watershed is land where rainwater runs off into streams. Streams feed into other streams, eventually building a river. **Bays** form along coastlines where wind and water have washed away weak rock, leaving behind solid, stronger rock under and around the water.

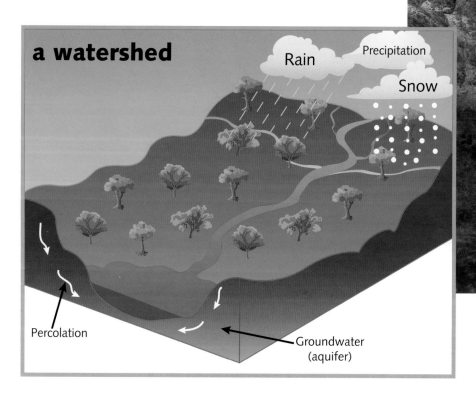

a watershed

Precipitation

Rain

Snow

Percolation

Groundwater
(aquifer)

Freezing and expansion of water also work to form canyons. Water seeps between cracks in rock and freezes, pushing and breaking the rock apart.

Rushing river waters drop rocks and mud called **sediment** into shallow water. Over time, the sediment can be pushed up, forming an island. Islands can also form from a build up of **magma** and ash after a volcano erupts. Peninsulas can form this way, too. Changing water levels can expose some land to make a peninsula.

Lakes are sometimes carved out by glaciers. Lakes can also form from spreading plate movement in Earth's crust.

Formed from the hollow of a glacier, Lake Bohinj is the largest natural permanent lake in Slovenia.

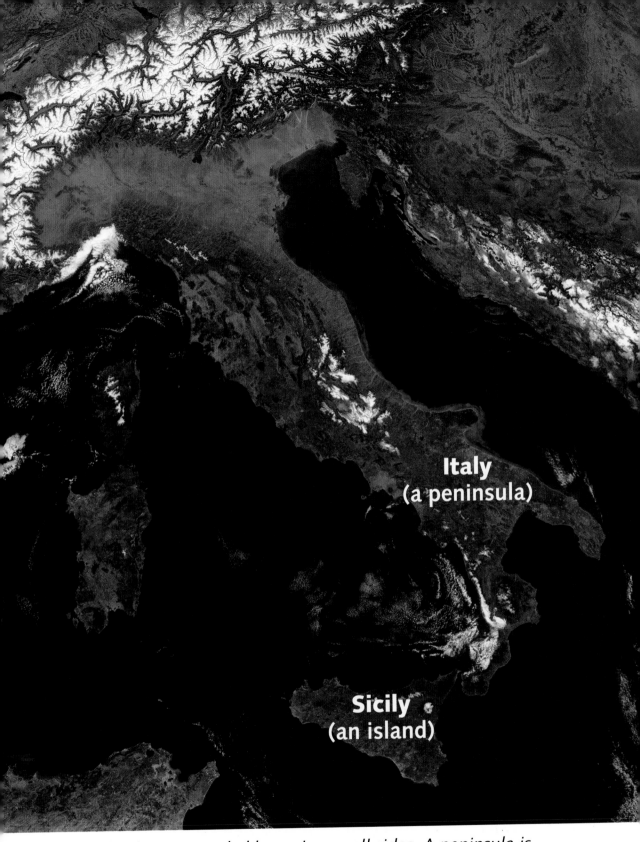

Italy
(a peninsula)

Sicily
(an island)

An island is surrounded by water on all sides. A peninsula is connected to mainland, but surrounded by water on 3 sides.

A plain is any low lying area that is level or that gently slopes. Plateaus are similar to plains, but are found at higher elevations and have at least one cliff-like side and a flattened top. Plains and plateaus can form from movement in Earth's crust or scraped flat by movement of ancient seas no longer there. Lava flow from a volcano can also shape plains and plateaus.

Grasslands cover dry plains like the Great Plains of the United States. Today, much of those grasslands furnish rich soil for crops.

The plateaus of Canyonlands National Park in Utah were carved by the Green and Colorado Rivers long ago.

Everyday, Earth's plates, along with wind and water, are hard at work shaping our landscape. Earth changes every day, inside and out!

Show What You Know

1. What is a scientist called that studies Earth inside and out?

2. Describe the three layers of Earth.

3. Name at least two forces that can change the shape of Earth.

Glossary

bays (bayz): parts of the sea that cut into the coastline and are partially enclosed by land

canyons (KAN-yuhnz): long, thin valleys with cliffs on both sides

core (kor): the center layer of the Earth

crust (kruhst): Earth's outer layer

geologists (jee-AH-luh-jistz): scientists who study Earth

glaciers (GLAY-shurz): large sheets of ice and snow that move slowly down mountains until they melt

lava (LA-vuh): melted rock flowing or thrown from a volcano

magma (MAG-muh): melted rock found under the Earth's surface

mantle (MAN-tuhl): Earth's moving middle layer

plates (playtz): sections of Earth's divided crust

sediment (SED-uh-muhnt): rock, sand, and mud set down by wind or water

Index

Websites to Visit

walrus.wr.usgs.gov/ask-a-geologist/

www.kidsgeo.com/geology-for-kids/0019-inside-of-earth.php

www.sciencenewsforkids.org/2008/09/where-rivers-run-uphill-2/

About the Author

Kimberly M. Hutmacher is the author of 24 books for children. She loves to research science topics and share what she learns. She also enjoys sharing her love of writing with audiences of all ages.

Ask The Author!
www.rem4students.com

24